Bloopers and

To…

May the Lord bless you and smile upon you today and always.

From…

Smile!

It exercises your face muscles.
It boosts your immune system.
It reduces stress.
It kills time between disasters.

A merry heart doeth good like a medicine…
Proverbs 17:22
(King James Version)

Signs of the Times...

Some churches put witty messages on their noticeboards.
Here are some of our favourites.

We are the soul agents in this area.

COME TO CHURCH THIS SUNDAY.
AVOID THE CHRISTMAS RUSH.

There are some questions that can't be answered by GOOGLE

CAN'T SLEEP?
DON'T COUNT SHEEP,
TALK TO THE SHEPHERD!

Hoot if you love Jesus.
Text while driving if you
want to meet him.

Over 2,000 years old
and still under the maker's guarantee.

Church Car Park
If you park here you are liable
1 To be blocked in
2 To be prayed for

If your problem
is long-standing,
try kneeling.

DOWN IN THE MOUTH?
COME IN FOR A
FAITH LIFT.

Don't let worry
kill you.
Let the church
help.

Church Bulletin Bloopers

Check out these extracts from church notice sheets!

Don't be surprised to find mistakes on your church notice sheet.
We print something for everyone and some people love finding mistakes.

★

Eight new choir robes are currently needed, due to the addition of several
new members and to the deterioration of some older ones.

The Women's Fellowship Group will start their spring
programme with a whine and cheese party.

The pastor would appreciate it if ladies could lend him their electric girdles
for the Shrove Tuesday Pancake Breakfast.

★

This year Ash Wednesday is on Thursday February the 10th.

★

Mrs Jones, our much-loved organism, will be retiring
at the end of next month.

7 of our 9 elders voted unanimously to purchase a new church minibus.

Mrs Johnson will be entering the hospital this week for testes.

★

Next week's fasting and prayer conference includes meals.

★

Diana and Don request your presents at their wedding.

Next Sunday we will all have the chance to eat and greet the candidates for elder.

The third verse of Blessed Assurance will be sung without musical accomplishment.

Crazy Christenings!

In 1900, the Duck family lived in Ramsbury Manor, England. When it was time for their third son to be christened the mother chose the name William. Unfortunately, the father was too ill with gout to go to the church, so he told the nanny to name him plain Bill. The nanny gave this name to the vicar and the poor baby was christened Plainbill Duck.

Many years ago a baby was taken to be christened in Peckham, South-East London. The parents and godparents arrived at the church, but they still hadn't agreed on a name. When the vicar said, "Please name this child," one friend said "John"; another disagreed saying "Oh no!" As no one else said anything, the poor baby was duly christened Ono Tichiner.

"I definitely want Brooklyn to be christened,
but I don't know into what religion yet."
Explained a certain famous footballer in a television interview!

A few years ago a popular baby website* conducted some research into 'The Most Unfortunate Names in Britain'. Here are their results...

Helen Back	Teresa Green
Terry Bull	Ray Gunn
Tim Burr	Doug Hole
Rose Bush	Jo King
Pearl Button	Lee King
Barry Cade	Hazel Nutt
Justin Case	Max Power
Mary Christmas	Will Power
Chris Cross	Stan Still
Sonny Day	Paige Turner
Barb Dwyer	Anna Sasin

* With thanks to
www.thebabywebsite.com

Out of the mouths of babes...

Two little girls were chatting,
"So, why don't you come to the same Sunday School as me?" said the first.
"Because I belong to a different abomination," replied the second.

❁

A Sunday School teacher was questioning her group,
"If I sell everything I have and give the money to the poor,
will that get me into heaven?"
"No," said her group.
"What about if I'm kind to animals and my neighbours?"
"No," said her group.
"And if I clean the church and help local charities,
will that get me into heaven?"
"No," said an earnest little girl, "you have to be DEAD!"

❁

One Sunday after church, a young boy announced to his mother,
"Mum, I'm going to be a minister when I grow up."
"Great, what made you decide that?"
"Well," said the little boy, "I have to go to church anyway, and I think it will be
more fun to stand up and shout than to sit still and listen."

A father was at the beach with his children when his 4-year-old son ran up to him, grabbed his hand, and led him to the shore, where a seagull lay dead in the sand.

"Daddy, what happened to him?" the son asked.

"He died and went to heaven," the dad replied.

The boy thought a moment and then said, "Did God throw him back down?"

❀

On a walkabout in Chichester, a few days before his enthronement, Archbishop Justin Welby was greeted by a party of smiling, waving schoolchildren. "Do you really know my name?" he asked.

"Justin Bieber" piped up an enthusiastic 7-year-old.

❀

At Sunday School Tom had heard the story of how Eve was created out of one of Adam's ribs. Later in the week he didn't feel at all well... "I have a pain in my side and I think I'm going to have a wife!"

❀

In the early 80s when 'wicked' and 'well wicked' meant something truly amazing, one little girl at a London holiday club drew a wonderful picture of Jesus. Under her picture, she wrote the caption 'Jesus is Wicked!'

Sunday School

Little children will be very important in heaven because they
will be the ones asking those extraordinary questions which are
so profound –
'But God, who made you?'
Archbishop Desmond Tutu, South African retired Anglican bishop,
1931–present day

❧

As they were going back into church for the last hymn, a Sunday School
teacher asked her group, "Do you think you could be really quiet?"
"Is that because people are sleeping?" asked one little girl.

❧

A Sunday School group had been learning the Ten Commandments and the
teacher asked if anyone could remember the last one. A little girl raised her
hand and answered, "Thou shall not take the covers off the neighbour's wife."

❧

After Sunday School, 4-year-old Carlton told his grandma the story
of Zacchaeus. "Do you think he was a nice man?" she asked.
"Oh no," he replied. "He stole everyone's taxes."
"And what do you think he did with them?" asked Gran.
"Well I expect he drove them!" said Carlton.

The Junior Church was hearing the story of the 'Good Samaritan', in which a man was beaten, robbed and left for dead. The group leader described the situation in vivid detail to keep the children's attention. Then she asked the class, "If you saw a person lying on the roadside all wounded and bleeding, what would you do?"

Eventually a little girl piped up, "I think I'd be sick."

&

A Sunday School teacher was describing how Lot's wife looked back at Sodom and immediately turned into a pillar of salt, when one little boy interrupted. "My mummy looked back once while she was driving," he announced, "and she turned into a telegraph pole."

Heather Hulett: Bath Abbey

Hands together and eyes closed...

A Sunday School group were all invited to write prayer letters to God. One little boy wrote, "Dear God. We had a lovely time at church today. Wish you could have been there."

"Sarah," said the group leader, "do you say your prayers every night?"
"No, not every night," she replied, "because sometimes
I don't want anything."

❖

Little Grace was very impressed when everyone was told to
"Stand for Grace" at the beginning of the wedding reception.

❖

A group of children in the nursery class were saying The Lord's Prayer
in assembly... "Our Father, who's Martin Evans, Hallowed be thy
name..." recited one 4-year-old. It turned out that there were three
boys called Martin in her class, so the mistake is easily understood.

❖

"Mummy," said a little girl, "I'm not going to finish my prayers with
Amen any more. I'm going to say RSVP."

❖

"Dear God," prayed a little lad. "I went to this wedding and they kissed
right in church. Is that OK with you? Amen."

❖

And finally, there are a few little ones who think God lives in
the south-west of England...
"Our Father, who art in Devon, Harold be thy name..."

Musical Misquotes!

These hymns and carols have all been misheard and misquoted by children.
Can you work out the original words?

♫

I've got the joy, joy, joy down in my heart Tuesday!
I got the pizza passes understanding...

♪

All things bright and beautiful, all teachers great and small.

♫

Dance, dance wherever you may be. I am the Lord of the dancing fleas.
I'll eat you all wherever you may be. I'll eat you all in the dance said he.

♪

Blessed insurance, Jesus is mine.
(The little boy's dad worked for an insurance company!)

♫

Lord, I lift your name on high...
You came from heaven to earth, to show the way.
From the earth to the cross, my dead toupee.

♪

In Morecambe, invisible, God only wise...

Hey! I knew ya, Hey! I knew ya, Give thanks to the risen Lord.
(A 2-year-old's rendition of 'Hallelujah! Hallelujah!')

Praise my soul the King of Heaven...
Praise the ever nasty King.
(Louise, aged 3, thought the last line was about Herod!)

♪

Get dressed you married gentlemen, let nothing you dismay.

♫

Crazy, crazy, all you little children...
('Praise him, Praise him' sung by a 3-year-old! His daddy thought this
version accurately described the situation.)

♪

Hark, the hairy angels sing,
Glory to the newborn thing...
Peace on earth and mercy mild
God and sinners wreck a child...
With the jelly toast proclaim
'Christ is born in Bethlehem!'

♫

O Come All Ye Faithful...
O come let us ignore him, O come let us ignore him,
O come let us ignore him, Christ the Lord.

The Wisdom of Youth

Hilarious exam howlers

In future, all cars will be fitted with Catholic converters.

▼

If someone dies in hospital, angels move them to the eternity ward.

▼

In the first book of the Bible, Guinessis, Adam and Eve were created from an apple tree.

▼

Joseph gave refuse to his brothers when they had a famine in Canaan.

▼

God created the world and then he created Adam and Ebay.

▼

God's people were called the Israel Lights.

▼

Moses led the Hebrew slaves to the Red Sea, where they made unleavened bread which is bread made without any ingredients.

▼

Samson slayed the Philistines with the axe of the Apostles.

In Jewish churches they don't have vickers, they have rabbits.

▼

David fought Goliath who was a very tall philatelist.

▼

The 5th commandment is humour thy father and mother.

▼

The epistles were the wives of the apostles.

▼

The people who followed the Lord were called the 12 decibels.

▼

Judaism has one big God named 'Yahoo'.

▼

The feminine of vicar is vixen.

▼

The end of the world will mark a turning point in everyone's life.

▼

The last book in the Bible is called The Book of Revolutions.

A Prayer for Commuters

Our Father who art in Hendon,
Harrow be thy name,
Thy Kingston come, thy Wimbledon,
In Erith as it is in Hendon.
Give us this day our daily Brent,
And forgive us our Westminsters,
as we forgive those who
Westminster against us.
Lead us not into Temple Station,
But deliver us from Ealing,
For thine is the Kingston,
The Purley and the Crawley,
For Esher and Esher,
Crouch End.

Anon

17th-Century Nun's Prayer

Lord, thou knowest better than I know myself that I am growing older
and will someday be old. Keep me from the fatal habit of thinking
I must say something on every subject and on every occasion.
Release me from craving to straighten out everybody's affairs.
Make me thoughtful but not moody; helpful but not bossy.
With my vast store of wisdom it seems a pity not to use it all,
but Thou knowest Lord, that I want a few friends at the end.

❖

Keep my mind free from the recital of endless details; give me wings
to get to the point. Seal my lips on my aches and pains.
They are increasing and love of rehearsing them is becoming sweeter
as the years go by. I dare not ask for grace enough to enjoy the tales
of other's pains, but help me to endure them with patience.

Judith Merrell: Whitby Abbey

I dare not ask for improved memory, but for a growing humility and a lessening cocksureness when my memory seems to clash with the memories of others. Teach me the glorious lesson that occasionally I may be mistaken.

❖

Keep me reasonably sweet; I do not want to be a saint – some of them are so hard to live with – but a sour old person is one of the crowning works of the Devil. Give me the ability to see good things in unexpected places and talents in unexpected people. And, give me, O Lord, the grace to tell them so.

Amen

Anon

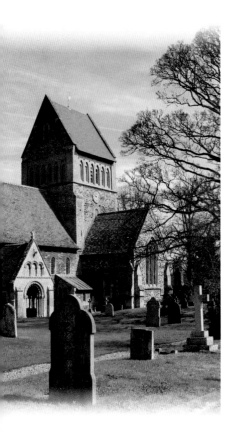

More Bulletin Bloopers!

A worm welcome to all who have come today.

★

While the vicar is on holiday, massages can be given to the church secretary.

★

For those of you who have children and don't know it, we have a crèche in the basement.

★

Weightwatchers will meet at 7pm. Please use the double doors at the back of the hall.

★

Men's Prayer Breakfast. No charge, but your damnation will be gratefully accepted.

Please place your donation in the envelope along with the deceased person you want remembered.

★

Remember the annual spring cleaning of the Parish Hall this Saturday. We need lots of volunteers to join the work crew. We have a long list of items to be cleaned and the widows will need extra attention.

★

Help blow up and decorate the church with balloons on Easter morning. Meet at 7.30am, won't take long.

★

For our Christingle service the pastor will light his candle from the altar candles. The ushers will light their candle from the pastor's candle. The ushers will turn and light each worshipper in the first pew.

★

During our opening harvest hymn, food, fruit and gifts of children can be laid on the altar.

★

A new loudspeaker system has been installed in the church. It was given by one of our members in honour of his wife.

★

Friday night. Bring and share meal. Prayer and Medication to follow.

Time for the Sermon...

A sermon should have a good beginning and a good end
and they should be as close together as possible.
George Burns, American comedian, 1896–1996

❖

A preacher once started his sermon with the words,
"I have so much to say I don't know where to begin."
A little boy piped up, "Could you start somewhere
near the end?"

❖

I don't mind if people look at their watches
while I'm preaching, but I get worried if they take
them off and shake them.

❖

When preaching of heaven let your face light up with
joy. When preaching of hell your ordinary face will do.
Charles Spurgeon, Baptist preacher, 1834–1892

❖

If all the people who fell asleep during sermons
were laid out end to end...
They would be a lot more comfortable!

A young vicar said to his wife, "Do I put enough fire into my sermons?" "Darling," she replied, "I don't think you put enough of your sermons in the fire."

❖

A minister was very worried about offending members of his church so his hesitant sermon went something like this: "Brethren, unless you repent, in a measure, and be converted, as it were, you will, I regret to say, be damned to some extent."

❖

The deeds you do today may be the only sermon some people will hear today.
Francis of Assisi, Italian Catholic friar, 1182-1226

❖

A mother finally discovered how to get her fidgety 7-year-old son to sit still and be quiet. About halfway through the sermon, she leaned over and whispered, "If you don't be quiet, the pastor is going to lose his place and will have to start his sermon all over again."

❖

Remember, to make a speech immortal you don't have to make it everlasting!

Brian Cartwright: St Andrew's Church, Colyton

25

Preachers and Pastors

Reverend Billy Graham tells of a time in his early ministry when he arrived in a small town to preach a sermon. Needing to post a letter, he asked a young boy the way to the post office. When the boy had told him, Dr. Graham thanked him and said, "If you come to the Baptist Church this evening, you can hear me telling everyone how to get to heaven."

The boy replied, "Thanks, but I don't think I'll bother... you don't even know your way to the post office."

Early one Sunday, a mother went in to wake her son.
"Wake up, son. It's time to go to Church!"
"No Mum, I don't want to go. The choir don't like me,
the congregation hate me and the sermons are boring!
Give me two reasons why I should go to church."
"Well son, for one, you're 55 years old. And for another, you're the vicar!"

Judith Merrell: Clerical Chasuble

An elderly vicar was not the best of drivers. One Sunday he was driving home from church when he had a minor bump with a cyclist. The poor man was knocked into the ditch. The vicar immediately stopped his car, got out and apologised, then he gave the cyclist his visiting card saying that if he ever needed help, the man should not hesitate to ask.

As the man rode home he looked at the card which said,
'The Reverend Johnston is sorry he missed you today.'

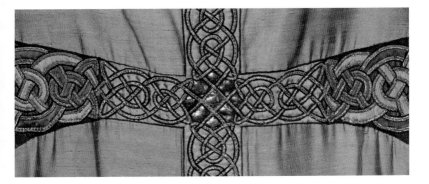

The new vicar's car broke down so he took it to the local garage on Monday. The mechanic identified the fault and said it would take a few days to fix.
"Please go easy on the costs," said the vicar, "I'm just a poor preacher."
"I know," said the mechanic, "I heard you yesterday."

Love and Marriage

Adam and Eve had an ideal marriage. He didn't have to hear about all
the men she could have married and she didn't have to hear how well
his mother cooked.

❤

Why does a woman work for ten years to change a man's habits
and then complain he's not the man she married?

Barbra Streisand, American singer and actress, 1942–present day

❤

Albert Einstein and his wife were interviewed on their golden wedding.
The reporter asked, "To what do you attribute the success of your marriage?"
"50 years ago we made a pact. In our life together, I would make all the big
decisions and she would make all the small ones. That, I think is the reason for
the success of our marriage." Then he added, "The strange thing is –
in 50 years there hasn't yet been one big decision."

❤

Signing the register at a wedding the best man couldn't make the
ballpoint pen work.
"Put your weight into it," said the vicar.
So he duly signed the book: John Smithson (11 stone 4 pounds).

After a quarrel, a wife said to her husband, "You know, I was a fool when I married you." He replied, "Yes dear, but I was in love and didn't notice."

❤

At the end of a wedding ceremony the Methodist minister raised his hand in order to give the final blessing. The nervous bride totally misunderstood this gesture and surprised the minister with a high-five. Not wanting to exclude the groom, the minister offered him a high-five as well and then gave the blessing while the congregation shook with laughter.

❤

At a wedding in Croydon, the bride and groom asked a friend to read
1 John Chapter 4: *God is love. Whoever lives in love lives in God,*
and God in them. Unfortunately the friend misheard and read
John 4, the story of 'The Woman at the Well', which includes these words:
You are right when you say you have no husband.
The fact is, you have had five husbands,
and the man you now have is not your husband...*
The bride and groom rocked with silent laughter
while the friend continued completely unaware.

*New International Version

Overheard at Church

A church was having difficulty getting people for the tea and coffee rota.
The ladies of the church said more men should help.
"Nonsense that's women's work," replied one gruff gentleman.
"Where does it say in the Bible that men should make the tea?"
One lady quietly opened the New Testament and pointed to Hebrews.

🐋

Young Darren was rather tired of the long sermon in church so he whispered
to his mother, "If we give him the money now, can we go?"

A young couple took their little daughter to a nativity service
to hear the story about Mary, Joseph and the baby Jesus.
Before the service they were enjoying refreshments in the church hall
and their little toddler was scrutinising the table of food,
"Mummy..." she said, "Where's the baby cheeses?"

❧

At a wedding, the Reverend William A. Spooner was heard to proclaim,
"It is kisstomary to cuss the bride."
And on another occasion he pronounced that,
"The Lord is a shoving leopard."

❧

"Two women called at my door and asked what bread I ate," said one woman
to another. "When I said white, they gave me a lecture on the benefits of
eating brown bread... I think they were both Hovis Witnesses!"

❧

"I don't understand why we always sing hims at church," said a little girl.
"Why can't we sing some hers?"

❧

"Vicar, we need to book a funeral with you," said a couple.
"We want a nice Christian burial, but nothing religious."

More Church Signs...

THIS CHURCH IS PRAYER-CONDITIONED.

God answers knee mail.

Seven days without prayer makes ONE WEAK.

DON'T WAIT for 6 strong men to take you to church.

Wireless communication is nothing new. This church has been praying for centuries.

COME WORK FOR THE LORD.
The work is hard, the hours are
long and the pay is low.
But the retirement benefits are
out of this world.

Faithbook
You have one
new friend
request from
Jesus.

And finally... this verse was pinned on
the door to the church crèche.

1 Corinthians 15:51
Behold, I tell you a mystery.
We will not all sleep,
but we will all be changed.

World English Bible

Who needs committees?

A committee is a group of the unprepared,
appointed by the unwilling, to do the unnecessary.
Fred Allen, American comedian, 1894-1956

❖

Church committees
consist of three types of people...
those who make things happen,
those who watch things happen and
those who haven't a clue what's happening.

❖

A committee is a group that keeps minutes and loses hours.
Milton Berle, American comedian, 1908–2002

Steve Harris: Normanton Church, Rutland Water

The vicar was recovering from an operation
and the curate came to visit him.
"How was the PCC meeting last night?"
"The good news is that we passed a vote to wish you
a speedy recovery and offer you this basket of fruit."
"And the bad news?"
"The vote was passed by seven votes to five."

❖

Nothing is accomplished by a committee unless
it consists of three members, one of whom is
sick and the other on holiday.

❖

God so loved the world
that he did not send a committee.

More Bulletin Bloopers!

The senior folks lunch club will no longer include lunch.

✤

Next Thursday there will be tryouts for the choir.
They need all the help they can get.

Last week we announced that Axxxx Nxxx had died. Many apologies –
we are very happy to say we were quite wrong.

Ladies, don't forget the rummage sale. It is a good chance to get rid of those
things not worth keeping around the house. Bring your husbands.

✤

Our harvest supper includes fine dining, super entertainment
and gracious hostility.

The Spring Retreat will be hell May 10th and 11th.

We are grateful for the help of those who cleaned up the grounds around
the church building and the rector.

Judith Merrell: Holy Trinity, Orton Longueville

Barbara remains in the hospital and needs blood donors for more transfusions. She is also having trouble sleeping and requests tapes of the pastor's sermons.

❖

Applications are now being accepted for 2-year-old crèche helpers.

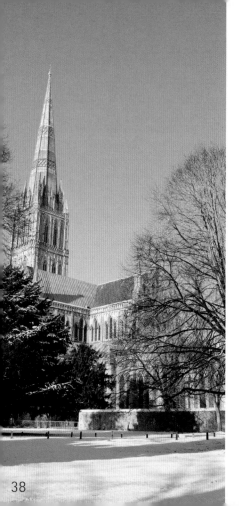

Christmas Crackers!

The nursery class were putting on the nativity play and the doll used at the rehearsal could not be found so a substitute was used. At the crucial moment in the performance the little girl playing Mary shouted, "STOP! This is the wrong baby!"

❅

One Christmas, the Sunday School heard the story of the shepherds visiting Mary, Joseph and baby Jesus in the stable and then they all drew pictures. One little boy included a dog in his nativity picture. When asked why, he explained that it was a German Shepherd.

The junior class had been learning the carol 'Born in a stable so bare' and afterwards they drew some pictures. One little lad had included Mary, Joseph, Jesus and a big brown blob at the back. "What's that?!" asked the teacher. "That's the stable bear, of course," replied the boy.

✳

After hearing about the Wise Men offering gifts to Jesus, one little boy said, "I know Jesus got money and gold when he was born, but I would have given him a Liverpool kit."

✳

A woman queued up for her Christmas stamps. "What denominations would you like?" asked the assistant. "Goodness, has it come to this? Give me five Methodist, 30 Church of England and 15 Baptist, please."

✳

Overheard at The Women's Fellowship Christmas party: "When it comes to choosing a Secret Santa gift, I'm going to pick the present I brought. That way I know I'll get something I like."

✳

A vicar was putting up a banner across the front of his church. In individual letters it spelt out GLORY TO GOD IN THE HIGHEST. Overnight, one of the letters fell down, so it read GLORY TO GOD IN THE HIGH ST. The vicar was going to replace the missing letter, until he realised that the banner spelt out a message that needed to be heard.

Famous Last Words

On his 75th birthday, Winston Churchill was asked how he felt about dying.
He replied, "I am ready to meet my Maker. Whether my Maker is prepared
for the great ordeal of meeting me is another matter."
These words were later engraved on his tombstone.

✠

"Some day," D.L. Moody used to say, "you will read in the papers that
D.L. Moody of East Northfield is dead. Don't believe a word of it! At that
moment I shall be more alive than I am now!"

✠

I read *The Times*, and if my name is not in the obits I proceed to enjoy the day.
Noel Coward, English playwright, 1899-1973 (attributed)

✠

I don't want to achieve immortality through my work...
I want to achieve it through not dying.
Woody Allen, American actor, director and writer, 1935–present day

✠

It's not that I'm afraid to die. I just don't want to be there when it happens.
Woody Allen

Reports of my death have been greatly exaggerated.

Mark Twain, American author, 1835–1910

✠

It was Bank Holiday weekend and there was a long queue to get petrol.
The garage attendant said, "If people know that they are going on a trip,
why do they always leave it until the last minute to get ready?"
"I know just what you mean," said the vicar. "It's like that in my job too."

✠

At the gates of heaven, Saint Peter looked at the new arrival,
somewhat puzzled. "How did you get here?" he asked.
"Flu!" came the immediate reply.

✠

When you look through the obituary columns in a newspaper,
isn't it amazing how people always die in alphabetical order?

Anon

Enlightening Epitaphs

The best is yet to come.
Frank Sinatra, 1915–1998, Cathedral City, California

❧

Dúirt mé leat go raibh mé breoite! - I told you I was ill!
Spike Milligan, Anglo-Irish comedian, 1918–2002, St Thomas' Church, Winchelsea, East Sussex

❧

A widow wrote this epitaph found in a Vermont cemetery:
Sacred to the memory of my husband John Barnes
who died January 3, 1803.
His comely young widow, aged 23, has many qualifications of a good wife,
and yearns to be comforted.

❧

She always said her feet were killing her but nobody believed her.
Margaret Daniels, Hollywood Cemetery, Richmond, Virginia

❧

When Christians see RIP
on a headstone,
we don't think Rest in Peace,
we think Rejoicing in Paradise.

I have sinned,
I have repented,
I have trusted,
I have loved,
I rest,
I shall rise,
And through the grace of Christ,
however unworthy,
I shall reign.
John Conder, 1714–1781,
Bunhill Fields, London

Here lies Ann Mann,
Who lived an old maid
But died an old Mann.
December 8, 1767,
London, England

Here lies
Johnny Yeast
Pardon me
For not rising.
Ruidoso Cemetery, New Mexico

Father God,

Help me to find joy in each new day,
and laughter in every adventure.
When I'm tempted to grumble and frown,
please nudge my funny bone
and tickle my ribs
until I see the funny side of the situation.

The LORD has done great things for us, and we are filled with joy.

Psalm 126:3

(New International Version)